olive

101 GLOBAL DISHES

D1408782

3 5 7 9 10 8 6 4 2

Published in 2007 by BBC Books,
an imprint of Ebury Publishing
A Random House Group Company

Copyright © Woodlands Books 2007

All photographs © **olive** magazine
All the recipes contained in this book first appeared in **olive** magazine

The Random House Group Limited Reg. No. 954009

Addresses for companies within the Random House Group can be found at
www.randomhouse.co.uk

A CIP catalogue record for this book is available from the British Library

The Random House Group Limited makes every effort to ensure that the
papers used in our books are made from trees that have been legally
sourced from well-managed and credibly certified forests. Our paper
procurement policy can be found on www.randomhouse.co.uk

Printed and bound by Firmengruppe APPL, aprinta druck, Wemding, Germany

ISBN: 9780563539032

olive

101 GLOBAL DISHES

classic dishes from around the world

Editor
Janine Ratcliffe

Contents

Introduction 6

Introduction

At **olive** we take our inspiration for recipes from all over the world; whether it's a dish eaten abroad, in a local restaurant or just a culinary style that's becoming more popular. With more and more global ingredients becoming widely available, it's never been easier to have a taste of the exotic every day.

Cooking food from other countries doesn't have to mean endless lists of unfamiliar ingredients and complicated methods. The recipes in this book use simple authentic flavours and techniques to capture the style of a country's food, so you won't have to spend all day shopping and cooking.

101 Global Dishes includes a style of cooking for every palate: so if you want a herb-infused Asian noodle soup, a spiced Indian curry, a nutty Middle-Eastern pilaf or a rich Italian ragu, then this is where you'll find them. For this collection the **olive** team have picked out easy and imaginative recipes like *Chicken tikka masala* pictured opposite (see page 116 for the recipe) that will satisfy the most adventurous of appetites.

As always, all the recipes have been thoroughly tested in the **olive** kitchen to make sure they taste fabulous and work for you first time.

Janine Ratcliffe
olive magazine

Notes and Conversions

NOTES ON THE RECIPES

• Where possible, we use humanely reared meats, free-range chickens and eggs, and unrefined sugar.

• Eggs are large unless stated otherwise. Pregnant women, elderly people, babies and toddlers, and anyone who is unwell should avoid eating raw and partially cooked eggs.

APPROXIMATE WEIGHT CONVERSIONS

• All the recipes in this book are listed with metric measurements.

• Cup measurements, which are used by cooks in Australia and America, have not been listed here as they vary from ingredient to ingredient. Please use kitchen scales to measure dry/solid ingredients.

OVEN TEMPERATURES

gas	°C	fan °C	°F	description
¼	110	90	225	Very cool
½	120	100	250	Very cool
1	140	120	275	Cool or slow
2	150	130	300	Cool or slow
3	160	140	325	Warm
4	180	160	350	Moderate
5	190	170	375	Moderately hot
6	200	180	400	Fairly hot
7	220	200	425	Hot
8	230	210	450	Very hot
9	240	220	475	Very hot

SPOON MEASURES

· Spoon measurements are level unless otherwise specified.

· 1 teaspoon (tsp) = 5ml

· 1 tablespoon (tbsp) = 15ml

· 1 Australian tablespoon = 20ml (cooks in Australia should measure 3 teaspoons where 1 tablespoon is specified in a recipe)

APPROXIMATE LIQUID CONVERSIONS

metric	imperial	US
60ml	2fl oz	¼ cup
125ml	4fl oz	½ cup
175ml	6fl oz	¾ cup
225ml	8fl oz	1 cup
300ml	10fl oz/½ pint	1¼ cups
450ml	16fl oz	2 cups/1 pint
600ml	20fl oz/1 pint	2½ cups
1 litre	35fl oz/1¾ pints	1 quart

Please note that an Australian cup is 250ml, ¾ cup is 190ml, ½ cup is 125ml, ¼ cup is 60ml.

Courgettes with feta and lemon thyme

20 minutes

courgettes 3 large
extra-virgin olive oil
lemon thyme 2 sprigs, chopped
feta 100g, crumbled

■ Heat the oven to 200C/fan 180C/gas 6. Shave the courgettes into strips using a potato peeler, or cut very finely on the diagonal. Toss in 2 tbsp olive oil, spread on a large baking sheet and scatter with the thyme.

■ Roast for 5 minutes, so the courgette still has some bite. Scatter with the feta and drizzle over 2 tbsp olive oil. **Serves 6**

Try this as part of a vegetarian meze: toss warm cooked potatoes with lemon rind and spring onions and serve alongside a fresh, grated carrot salad sprinkled with coriander leaves and sesame oil.

Grilled fig, pecan and halloumi salad

30 minutes

halloumi 200g block, sliced into 6
fresh figs 9, halved
rocket 150g
pecan halves 50g, roughly chopped

DRESSING
olive oil 3 tbsp
lemon juice 1 tbsp
rose harissa 2 tbsp, or use plain harissa
coriander leaves 1 tbsp, chopped

■ Heat a grill pan (chargrill) until very hot, cook the halloumi for a few minutes each side until golden. Remove and keep warm.
■ Brush the figs with a little olive oil. Put them cut-side down on the grill pan and cook for 2–3 minutes. Remove carefully.
■ Whisk all the dressing ingredients together in a bowl and season. Divide the rocket among six serving plates and top with the halloumi and figs. Scatter the pecans over and drizzle with the dressing.
Serves 6

Halloumi is a hard cheese that can be grilled, griddled or fried without losing its shape; you can find it in most supermarkets.

Chorizo and pork belly with haricot beans

20 minutes + 2 ½ hours in the oven

boneless pork belly 750g piece, skin removed

olive oil

diced pancetta 130g

onion 1 large, chopped

garlic 2 cloves, roughly chopped

hot smoked paprika 1 tsp

chorizo 200g, roughly chopped

chopped tomatoes 400g tin

red wine 150ml

haricot or **cannellini beans** 400g tin, drained and rinsed

coriander leaves a bunch, roughly chopped

You can also use dried beans; they'll need about 8 hours soaking in cold water, followed by about 30 minutes to 1 hour at a simmer, depending on the age of the bean (the older they are, the drier they'll be).

■ Heat the oven to 160C/fan 140C/gas 3. Cut the pork belly into large chunks. Heat 1 tbsp oil in a large, ovenproof casserole and fry the pork in batches over a high heat until browned all over, then remove with a slotted spoon.

■ Add the pancetta and cook for 2–3 minutes until golden, then reduce the heat slightly and add the onion and garlic. Cook for 2–3 minutes until softened. Stir in the paprika and chorizo and cook for a minute or so. Return the pork to the pan and tip in the tomatoes. Pour in the wine and enough water just to cover – about 350ml. Season, cover and cook in the oven for 2 hours.

■ Stir in the haricot beans and return to the oven, without the lid, for 20–30 minutes. Stir in the coriander and serve with crusty bread. **Serves 6**

Gnocchi with asparagus

20 minutes

asparagus 1 large bunch, about 250g, trimmed
gnocchi 500g
Boursin or **herbed cream cheese**, 150g
lemon 1, zested
parmesan 2 tbsp, freshly grated
parsley leaves 1 tbsp, chopped

■ Bring 2 pans of salted water to the boil and heat the grill to its highest setting. Cut the asparagus into 3–4cm lengths, keeping the tips separate. Put the asparagus stems into the boiling water and cook for 2 minutes, then add the tips and cook for a further 2 minutes. Drain thoroughly.

■ Meanwhile, cook the gnocchi in the other pan: they're ready when they float to the surface. Drain.

■ Put the cream cheese in a pan with 8 tbsp water and the lemon zest. Stir together over a medium heat until the cheese melts to a creamy sauce. Season.

■ Stir in the gnocchi and asparagus, and pile into a shallow heatproof dish. Scatter over the parmesan and parsley and brown under the grill. **Serves 2**

Cream cheese with herbs or garlic makes a brilliant and quick cheat's sauce.

Greek baked lamb with olives

1 hour

olive oil 2 tbsp
onion 1 large, finely sliced
garlic 4 cloves, chopped
lamb shoulder steaks 4 × 150g
potatoes 900g, cut into chunks
cherry tomatoes or **chopped tomatoes**
   1 × 400g tin
lamb or **beef stock** fresh, cube or
   concentrate, made up to 600ml
bay leaf 1
dried oregano 2 tsp
pitted kalamata olives 125g
caper berries or **capers** 25g, rinsed
fresh oregano a small bunch, roughly
   chopped

■ Heat the oven to 180C/fan 160C/gas 4. Heat the oil in a large roasting tin. Add the onion and garlic and cook for a few minutes. Push the onions and garlic to one side, then add the lamb steaks and brown for a few minutes on each side. Add the potatoes with the tomatoes, lamb or beef stock, bay leaf, dried oregano, olives and caper berries and stir well. Season.

■ Bake for 40 minutes, until the lamb is tender and the potatoes are cooked and the stock reduced. Scatter on the fresh oregano and serve with a salad. **Serves 4**

Make up a quick salad to go with this with little gem lettuce, finely sliced red onion, roughly chopped fresh mint and crumbled feta cheese.

Greek-style chickpea and parsley salad

10 minutes

chickpeas 400g tin, drained and rinsed

red onion ½, cut into thin wedges

cucumber ¼, halved lengthways and sliced diagonally

flat-leaf parsley leaves a small bunch, roughly chopped

feta 100g, crumbled

basil leaves a small handful, shredded

red wine vinegar 2 tbsp

extra-virgin olive oil 3 tbsp

■ Put the chickpeas, onion, cucumber, parsley, feta and basil in a large bowl and toss well to combine. Mix the red wine vinegar and extra-virgin olive oil together and season well. Pour over the salad and toss. **Serves 2**

Eat this on its own or with houmous and warm pitta bread.

Griddled marinated aubergine with feta and herbs

20 minutes

aubergines 2 large, sliced lengthways into ½cm-thick slices

olive oil

lemon 1, juiced

garlic 1 clove, crushed

feta 200g, crumbled

flat-leaf parsley leaves a large handful, finely chopped

coriander leaves a large handful, finely chopped

■ Heat a griddle or frying pan until very hot. Brush the aubergine with a little oil and griddle or fry in batches until soft and cooked through. Arrange on a platter.

■ Mix together the lemon and garlic with 5 tbsp olive oil and some seasoning, and drizzle over the aubergine. Let the flavours meld together for 5 minutes, then scatter the feta and herbs over and serve. **Serves 4**

Always oil the vegetables to be grilled, not the griddle pan. That way your kitchen won't be filled with smoke.

Halloumi wrapped in red pepper with lemon and chilli

30 minutes

red peppers 4
halloumi 200g block, sliced into 4
lemon 1, zested and juiced
red chilli 1, finely chopped
fresh oregano chopped to make 2 tsp
　　or **dried**, 1 tsp
black or **green olives** 4, cut into slivers

You can use ready-roasted peppers for speed – just look for large ones.

■ Grill or roast the red peppers whole until they begin to soften. You need them soft enough to wrap the cheese but not too soft or you won't be able to cook them again.

■ Open out each red pepper by making a cut down one side and trim the tops and bottoms. Put a slice of halloumi in the centre of each. Sprinkle over some lemon zest and juice, divide the chilli, oregano and olives among them, then roll the red pepper around the halloumi. Tie the rolls with some kitchen string that you have soaked in water (or secure with a cocktail stick) and press down with the palm of your hand so they flatten slightly.

■ Barbecue or grill the red peppers on both sides for 5 minutes or until they are starting to char and the cheese is softening and browning at the ends (keep an eye on the string as it could burn off). **Serves 4**

Mozzarella and artichoke panini

10 minutes

artichoke hearts 8 (from the deli counter or out of a jar)
ciabatta 4 long slices, cut diagonally from a large loaf
semi-dried tomatoes in olive oil 4
basil leaves a good handful
mozzarella 125g ball, sliced
olive oil from the semi-dried tomatoes

■ Cut 4 of the artichoke hearts into quarters. Whiz the rest to a paste in a food processor. Spread the artichoke paste on 2 slices of ciabatta. Cover with artichokes, tomatoes and basil, then mozzarella. Season with salt and pepper; cover with remaining bread.
■ Drizzle both sides sparingly with oil. Cook on a hot griddle pan (or heavy-based frying pan) for 2 minutes each side. **Serves 2**

Cow's-milk mozzarella is fine for melting – it's less expensive than buffalo mozzarella and its elastic texture is perfect for pizzas, pastas and toasted sandwiches.

Courgettes, garlic and chilli pasta

20 minutes

linguine 200g
olive oil 1 tbsp
courgettes 4, finely sliced
red chilli 1 long one, shredded
garlic 2 cloves, crushed
lemon 1, halved

■ Cook the pasta following the packet instructions. Meanwhile, heat the olive oil in a non-stick pan and fry the courgettes with the chilli and garlic until they brown nicely. Season well.

■ Divide the pasta between two bowls and then top with the courgettes and squeeze a lemon half over. **Serves 2**

Keep a jar of dried chilli flakes in your cupboard and use a big pinch in place of fresh chilli in cooking.

Pasta with steak, tomatoes and olives

20 minutes

spaghetti 150g

sirloin steak 200g

sugar snap peas 100g

cherry tomatoes 100g

red onion ½ small, finely sliced

olive oil 2 tbsp

black olives 12

flat-leaf parsley leaves a small bunch, chopped

red chilli 1, finely sliced

rocket 100g

basil leaves a handful

parmesan 50g, shaved

■ Bring a large pan of water to the boil, add the spaghetti and cook for 8 minutes. Put the steak on top of the pasta, reduce the heat, cover and simmer for 2 minutes for rare or 4 minutes for medium. If you want your steak well done, add to the pasta after 6 minutes and cook for 6 minutes.

■ Add the sugar snaps, tomatoes and onion, cover and simmer gently for a further 1 minute.

■ Transfer the steak to a board. Drain the pasta mixture, then return to the pan with the olive oil, olives, parsley, chilli and rocket. Season and mix well.

■ Slice the steak thinly with a sharp knife and stir into the pasta. Scatter torn basil leaves and parmesan shavings on top.

Serves 2

Use a potato peeler to get long shavings from a block of parmesan.

Rosemary chicken with tomato and chickpea salad

20 minutes

chicken breasts 2, sliced horizontally
and butterflied
lemon 1, juiced
rosemary needles from 2 sprigs, chopped
chickpeas 400g tin, drained and rinsed
red onion ½, sliced
cherry tomatoes 12, halved
olive oil 2 tsp

■ Put the chicken breasts in a dish with half the lemon juice and the rosemary. Season and leave for 10 minutes. Toss the chickpeas with the red onion, tomatoes, rest of the lemon juice and the olive oil.

■ Griddle (chargrill) or grill the chicken for about 5 minutes each side until cooked through. Serve with the chickpea salad. **Serves 2**

To butterfly chicken breasts, slice through horizontally, open out like a book then roll with a rolling pin to flatten slightly.

Spanish baked prawns

20 minutes

raw king prawns 300g, peeled and
  de-veined
garlic 2 cloves, thinly sliced
dried chilli flakes a large pinch
dry sherry 2 tbsp, fino is good
olive oil 2 tbsp
parsley leaves a small handful, chopped

■ Heat the oven to 220C/fan 200C/gas 7.
Divide the prawns, garlic, chilli, sherry
and the olive oil between 2 small
ovenproof dishes. Cook for 6–8 minutes
until pink and sizzling. Sprinkle with the
parsley and serve with crusty bread.
Serves 2

Raw prawns deteriorate very quickly –
when buying, avoid any that smell
particularly fishy.

Tomato and pesto tart

40 minutes

ready-rolled puff pastry 1 sheet
pesto 4 tbsp
mascarpone 2 tbsp
vine tomatoes 6, thinly sliced

■ Heat the oven to 200C/fan 180C/gas 6. Unroll the pastry on to a baking sheet and score a border 1cm from the edge. Prick inside the border with a fork, then bake for 15–20 minutes until light golden.
■ Gently squash down the middle. Spread the pesto inside the border, dot over the mascarpone, then layer the tomato on top. Season. Bake for 10 minutes until the tomatoes are cooked and the mascarpone has melted. **Serves 4**

Buy British tomatoes when in season – there are loads of different varieties to choose from.

Pesto and potato tart

45 minutes

new potatoes 400g, thinly sliced
ready-rolled shortcrust pastry 1 sheet
pesto 2–3 tbsp
parmesan 3 tbsp, freshly grated
egg 1, beaten
basil leaves a small handful

■ Heat the oven to 190C/fan 170C/gas 5. Simmer the potato slices for 2 minutes and drain. Put the pastry on a baking sheet and fold in the edges to make a border.

■ Spread a thin layer of pesto over the base and sprinkle the parmesan over. Lay the potato slices on top. Season. Glaze the borders with the egg. Bake for 25–30 minutes until the pastry is golden and crisp and the potatoes tender. Sprinkle with basil to serve. **Serves 4**

Classic pesto is made with basil, pine nuts, garlic, olive oil and parmesan. Cheaper versions use cashew nuts and vegetable oil, so check the label when buying.

Veal saltimbocca

20 minutes

veal escalopes 2, about 150g each
prosciutto 2 slices
sage leaves 2
lemon 2 slices
plain flour 1 tbsp
olive oil and butter for frying
dry (secco) marsala 200ml
polenta or mashed potato to serve

■ Put each escalope between pieces of clingfilm and, using a rolling pin, roll them out to a thickness of about 5mm. Season. Lay a slice of prosciutto on top of each escalope and put a sage leaf on top of that. Cover the sage with a slice of lemon and secure the whole thing with a cocktail stick. Lightly dust with flour on both sides.

■ Heat a little oil and a knob of butter in a frying pan. Cook the veal for about 3 minutes on each side until golden brown and cooked through. Add the marsala to the pan and bubble until thickened and reduced by about half. Season and serve with either mashed potatoes or creamy polenta. **Serves 2**

You can also make this with chicken fillets: make a deep horizontal cut into the fillet, open it out like a book and then roll it out like the veal, as described here.

Lemon pannacotta with lemon caramel

30 minutes + cooling and setting

sunflower oil for greasing
full-fat milk 375ml
double cream 375ml
lemon 1, zested in thick strips
caster sugar 100g
gelatine 2 tsp powdered or 4 leaves
soaked in cold water

LEMON CARAMEL
caster sugar 100g
lemon juice 1 tbsp (from the zested
lemon)

Caramel behaves better if it is made in a stainless-steel rather than non-stick pan. It's also easier to see the colour change.

■ Brush 6 150ml pudding moulds with a little sunflower oil. Put the milk and cream in a saucepan. Add the lemon zest and sugar, bring slowly to the boil then remove from the heat.

■ Pour 150ml of the milk mix into a small bowl, add the gelatine and stir until it has completely dissolved. Leave the rest of the mixture to cool to room temperature and infuse with the zest. Stir the 2 mixtures together and strain through a fine sieve into the moulds. Chill until set.

■ Meanwhile, to make the caramel, heat the sugar in a saucepan until it melts and turns a golden colour – you may need to swirl the pan to keep the colour even. Take off the heat and add the lemon juice – it will splutter. Re-melt the caramel if it has hardened in lumps and then drizzle on to a piece of baking parchment on a chopping board. Cool and break into pieces. Serve the pannacotta turned out on to plates and topped with the caramel pieces. **Makes 6**

Vanilla gelato

20 minutes + freezing

egg yolks 5
caster sugar 225g
milk 500ml
single cream 125ml
vanilla extract 1 tsp
vanilla pod 1, cut into thin strips

Vanilla extract is made from real vanilla seeds – avoid vanilla essence, which is an artificial flavouring.

■ Whisk the egg yolks and sugar in a large bowl until the mixture is thick and pale yellow. Heat the milk to a simmer then whisk it into the egg mixture. Pour back into the pan (rinse it out first) and cook over a low heat, stirring constantly until the mixture is thick enough to coat the back of a spoon. Don't boil or it will scramble. Stir in the cream and vanilla extract and cool.

■ Strain into an ice-cream maker (or freezer box) and churn until frozen (or freeze). Serve scoops in chilled glasses decorated with a vanilla-pod strip.

Serves 6

Bulghar wheat with feta and pomegranate

30 minutes

bulghar wheat 200g

harissa 1 tsp

feta 200g

pomegranate 1, seeds only

carrot 1, coarsely grated

red onion ½ small, sliced

cooked beetroot 100g, cut into
   matchsticks

mint leaves chopped to make 3 tbsp

lemon cut into wedges, to serve

■ Put the bulghar wheat into a bowl and just cover with boiling water. Leave for about 10–15 minutes to soften and absorb the water. Drain off any excess. Stir in the harissa paste and season.

■ Meanwhile, crumble the feta into a bowl with the pomegranate seeds. Mix in the carrot and onion. Add to the bulghar wheat and toss together. Divide the mixture among 4 plates. Scatter with the beetroot and mint and serve with lemon wedges. **Serves 4**

To get the pomegranate seeds, cut a cross in the top, then tear the fruit into quarters. The seeds will pop out as you tear, so do so over a bowl.

Chickpea and pomegranate dip with pitta crisps

30 minutes

pitta breads 6–8

extra-virgin olive oil 100ml, plus extra for the crisps

chickpeas 3 × 400g tins, drained

lemon 1, juiced

red chillies 2, seeded and chopped

garlic 1 clove, finely chopped

cumin seeds 2 tsp, toasted in a dry frying pan

red onion 1 small, finely chopped

mint leaves or parsley leaves a small bunch, finely chopped

pomegranate molasses or tamarind paste thinned down with water, 2 tbsp

■ Heat the oven to 200C/fan 180C/gas 6. Cut the pittas into triangles and separate the layers. Brush with olive oil, season and bake for 7–8 minutes until crisp and golden.

■ Put the chickpeas, 100ml olive oil, lemon juice, chilli and garlic in a food processor, season and pulse until just crushed. Remove and mix in the cumin seeds, red onion and mint or parsley. Season. Drizzle with pomegranate molasses and serve with warm pitta crisps. **Serves 8**

You can buy pomegranate molasses, a sweet and sour syrup, at some supermarkets or a Middle-Eastern grocer.

Houmous

10 minutes

chickpeas 1 × 400g tin
tahini 3 tbsp
garlic 1 clove, crushed
lemon 1, juiced
olive oil 3 tbsp
ground cumin 1 tsp
pitta breads to serve

■ Put the chickpeas into a food processor and whiz briefly. Add the rest of the ingredients and 3 tbsp water. Whiz again until you get the consistency you like (you can add a little more water if you prefer it smoother).

■ Season well and put into a serving bowl. Drizzle over some olive oil and serve with warm pitta breads. **Serves 4**

Add more lemon juice, garlic or a little pinch of chilli powder, depending on your taste.

Grilled lamb cutlets with mint and apricot couscous

20 minutes

couscous 1 cupful
dried apricots a handful, roughly chopped
harissa 1–2 tsp
lamb cutlets 6 small, trimmed of all fat
mint leaves 1 bunch, chopped
parsley leaves 1 bunch, chopped

■ Tip the couscous into a bowl with the apricots and half the harissa and add 1 ½ cupfuls of boiling water. Cover and leave to swell for 5 minutes.

■ Meanwhile, rub the lamb all over with the rest of the harissa and grill for 3 minutes on each side or until it is cooked through. Stir the mint and parsley through the couscous and serve with the lamb. **Serves 2**

Harissa is a hot paste from Morocco, made with chillies, spices and garlic. Buy it ready-made in jars from the spice section.

Lamb kebabs

40 minutes

lamb leg steaks 4 large, cut into chunks
ground cumin 1 tsp
chilli powder 1 tsp
garlic 1 clove, crushed
lemon 1, juiced
red cabbage ½, finely shredded
red onion ½, finely sliced
pitta breads 4

YOGHURT SAUCE
thick natural yoghurt 200ml
cucumber ¼, seeds removed and grated
garlic ½ clove, crushed (optional)

■ Toss the lamb with the cumin, chilli, garlic and 1 tbsp lemon juice. Season and leave for 20 minutes. Toss the cabbage and onion with the rest of the lemon juice and a good pinch of salt. Thread the lamb on to skewers and grill or chargrill for 3–4 minutes each side. Mix the yoghurt with the cucumber and garlic (if using) and season. Warm the pittas, split and fill with cabbage mix. Divide the lamb among the pittas and top with yoghurt sauce. **Serves 4**

This is a shish, not doner, kebab so it's made with grilled, marinated cubes of lamb instead of slices.

Lamb sausages on rosemary skewers

15 minutes

lamb sausages 8
rosemary 8 long sprigs, preferably
    slightly woody
mint leaves a handful, chopped
Greek yoghurt 200ml
pitta breads 8

You need quite hard, long sprigs of rosemary for this – or you can use wooden skewers soaked in water for half an hour.

■ Push a sausage lengthways on to each rosemary sprig (it might be easier if you make a hole in the sausages first with a skewer). Mix the mint and yoghurt and season well.

■ Heat a barbecue or grill and cook the sausage skewers on both sides until browned and cooked through. How long this takes will depend on what kind of barbecue you have, but don't overcook the sausages or the rosemary will burn. Lightly toast the pittas on the barbecue. Serve the sausages with the pittas and the minted yoghurt. **Serves 4**

Moroccan tuna kebabs with couscous

20 minutes

tuna steaks 2, cut into large chunks
harissa 2 tbsp, plus extra to serve
lemons 2, 1 juiced, 1 cut into wedges
vegetable stock fresh, cube or
    concentrate, made up to 200ml, hot,
    mixed with 1 tsp **ground cumin**
couscous 100g
mint leaves a small bunch, roughly
    chopped

■ Toss the tuna with the harissa and
1 tbsp lemon juice and leave for
10 minutes. Pour the stock over the
couscous. Cover, leave for 5 minutes, then
fluff with a fork.

■ Thread the tuna on to 4 skewers and
grill for a minute each side. Mix the rest
of the lemon juice and the mint with the
couscous. Serve with the tuna kebabs and
lemon wedges and a little extra harissa
on the side. **Serves 2**

Buying pole-and-line-caught tuna means
it has been responsibly fished without
harming other sea life.

Red mullet with chermoula

15 minutes + marinating time

flat-leaf parsley leaves a handful, finely
    chopped
coriander leaves a handful, finely
    chopped
garlic 2 cloves, crushed
paprika 1 tsp
ground cumin 1 tsp
lemon 1, zest and juice
olive oil 6 tbsp
red mullet 4 large or 8 small fillets,
    skin on

■ To make the chermoula, mix the herbs, garlic, spices, lemon zest and juice and oil and a good pinch of salt flakes. Put the red mullet in a dish in a single layer and pour over the chermoula. Leave to marinate for up to 1 hour.

■ Heat the grill to hot. Lift the fillets out of the marinade and put them on an oiled baking sheet skin-side up. Grill until browned. Pour over any extra marinade and flash back under the grill briefly.

Serves 4

Leave the skin on the red mullet and it will look much prettier and help the fillets to stay intact while grilling.

Roasted beets with feta and cumin

1 hour

---

beetroot 500g small, halved

olive oil 2 tbsp

cumin seeds 2 tsp

feta 200g, broken into chunks

dried chilli flakes a sprinkle

■ Heat the oven to 200C/fan 180C/gas 6. Put the beets in a baking dish flat-side up. Heat the oil and the cumin in a frying pan, cook until it sizzles and then pour over the beets. Season and bake for 30 minutes. Dot the feta among the beets, sprinkle some chilli flakes over and bake for another 20 minutes. **Serves 4**

Always roast beetroot with the skin on to keep in all the juices and flavour.

Roasted red peppers and aubergines with goat's cheese

20 minutes

roasted red peppers 3 large, drained

soft goat's cheese 125g

grilled aubergines in oil 150g, drained

semi-dried tomatoes 4, chopped (try Merchant Gourmet, either Mi-Cuit or SunBlush)

basil leaves a handful, torn

rocket a handful

extra virgin olive oil and balsamic vinegar to drizzle

ciabatta toasted, to serve

■ Slice each red pepper in half and spread each piece with goat's cheese. Top with a slice of aubergine, some tomato and basil. Season with salt and pepper and roll up.

■ Divide the pepper rolls between two plates. Garnish with the rocket and drizzle with olive oil and balsamic vinegar. Serve with toasted ciabatta.

Serves 2

Buy the roasted red peppers and grilled aubergines from deli counters or in jars (Karyatis is a good brand).

Runner beans with tomato and oregano

40 minutes

runner beans 450g

olive oil for frying

red onion 1, finely sliced

garlic 2 cloves, sliced

turmeric 2 tsp

kalonji (black onion seeds) 2 tsp

fresh oregano 2 sprigs

cherry or plum tomatoes 2 × 400g tins

■ Snap the ends off the beans and pull off any strings from the outside edges. Slice the beans diagonally.

■ Heat a good slug of oil in a deep frying pan, add the onion and garlic and cook over a low heat for about 4 minutes until tender but not browned. Add the spices and stir. Add the oregano and tomatoes and bring to the boil. Add the beans, cover and reduce heat to a simmer. Cook for 30 minutes or until the beans are tender – they won't be bright green by now. Season well. **Serves 6**

You can find kalonji seeds in major supermarkets and Indian shops.

Spinach, mushroom and lemon pilaf

30 minutes

onions 2, finely sliced
garlic 2 cloves, crushed
butter 50g
chestnut mushrooms 150g, sliced
cinnamon 1 stick
cloves 4 whole
cardamom pods 4 bruised
basmati rice 250g
lemon ½, zested and juiced
vegetable stock fresh, cube or
    concentrate, made up to 450ml
spinach 200g, washed and roughly
    chopped

■ Cook the onion and garlic in the butter in a large, shallow pan until soft and golden. Add the mushrooms and cook until softened. Add the spices and cook for 2 minutes, then stir in the rice, lemon zest and stock. Cover. Cook on a gentle heat for about 15 minutes until the liquid has been absorbed. Stir through the spinach and lemon juice, cover for 2 minutes until wilted and serve. **Serves 4**

To wilt spinach quickly, put it in a colander and pour over a kettle of boiling water.

Spicy lamb and prunes on pistachio couscous

30 minutes

---

ready-to-eat prunes 100g, roughly
    chopped
couscous 100g
vegetable stock fresh, cube or
    concentrate, made up to 150ml, hot
lamb neck fillet 350g, cut into thick slices
harissa 1 tbsp
pistachio nuts 50g, shelled and roughly
    chopped
mint leaves a handful, chopped
lemon wedges to serve

■ Put the prunes in a mug and just cover with boiling water. Put the couscous in a bowl, pour the hot stock over, cover and put to one side. Mix the lamb with the harissa.

■ Heat a dry frying pan and cook the pistachios until just starting to brown. Tip them out of the pan and add the lamb. Fry for 2–3 minutes each side, until well browned. Add the prunes and their water and bubble up, stirring and scraping until the lamb is cooked through.

■ Mix the pistachios with the couscous and serve topped with the lamb and prunes and mint, with the lemon wedges to squeeze over. **Serves 2**

Ready-to-eat prunes are much softer and juicier than regular dried ones, which will need longer soaking time.

Stuffed peppers with rice, pine nuts and dill

50 minutes

olive oil 2 tbsp, plus extra for drizzling

onion 1, finely chopped

pine nuts 4 tbsp

smoked paprika 1 tsp

ground cinnamon 1 tsp

basmati rice 125g, cooked

fresh dill 4 tbsp, chopped

feta 100g, cubed

peppers, **orange**, **red** or **yellow** 2, halved

■ Heat the oven to 180C/fan 160C/gas 4. Heat the olive oil in a frying pan and cook the onion over a low heat until golden. Add the pine nuts and brown lightly. Stir in the spices and cook for a minute. Add the cooked rice and dill and stir together. Season well. Fold in the feta.

■ Put the peppers, cut-side up, in a shallow baking dish or roasting tin. Divide the mixture among them and drizzle liberally with olive oil. Cover with foil and roast for 40 minutes until the peppers are tender, then remove the foil and cook for a further 5 minutes. **Serves 2**

You can serve these peppers, hot or cold, as part of a picnic or buffet.

Tabbouleh

35 minutes

bulghar wheat 120g
spring onions 3, finely sliced
cherry tomatoes 200g, halved or
   quartered
mint leaves 2 big bunches, chopped
parsley leaves 1 bunch, chopped
lemons 2, zest and juice
olive oil
little gem lettuces to serve

■ Soak the bulghar in boiling water for 30 minutes – cover with a couple of centimetres of water. When it is soft, rinse it in cold water and drain well.
■ Mix the bulghar with the spring onions, cherry tomatoes, mint and parsley. Stir in the lemon zest and juice, season well and add a good slug of oil. Pile the tabbouleh on to a platter and serve with the little gem lettuce leaves around the edge to use as scoops. **Serves 4**

Classic tabbouleh has a good proportion of herbs to bulghar wheat, so make sure you get decent-sized bunches.

Vegetable tagine with toasted almond couscous

1 hour 15 minutes

olive oil 2 tbsp

onions 2, thinly sliced

ground cumin and ground coriander 2 tsp
of each

garlic 2 cloves, finely sliced

harissa 3 tbsp

butternut squash 1 small, peeled and cut
into chunks

carrots 4, cut into chunks

vegetable stock fresh, cube or
concentrate, made up to 600ml

ready-to-eat dried apricots 75g, chopped

chickpeas 400g tin, drained and rinsed

flat-leaf parsley a bunch, roughly chopped

coriander leaves a bunch, roughly
chopped

COUSCOUS

couscous 300g

vegetable stock fresh, cube or
concentrate, made up to 600ml

flaked almonds 4 tbsp, toasted

■ Heat the oil in a tagine or casserole and gently cook the onion until soft – about 10 minutes. Add the ground spices and garlic and cook for a minute. Stir in the harissa and cook for 2 minutes. Stir through the squash and carrots and toss well. Pour over the stock, add the apricots and bring to a gentle simmer. Cook over a low heat for about 25–30 minutes until the vegetables are very tender.

■ Meanwhile, put the couscous in a large bowl, bring the stock to the boil and pour it over. Cover the bowl and leave to stand for 5–10 minutes. Gently fluff up with a fork and stir through the toasted almonds. Add the chickpeas to the tagine and stir through half of the herbs. Season, then simmer for 5 minutes. Spoon the couscous into bowls then ladle the tagine on top. Serve scattered with extra herbs.

Tagines are named after the conical ceramic pots in which they are traditionally cooked. A casserole dish is a good substitute.

Garlicky potato and mushroom gratin

1 hour

waxy potatoes 450g, such as Charlotte, peeled

Portobello mushrooms 150g, thickly sliced

olive oil for frying

bay leaf 1

double cream 200ml

milk 100ml

Dijon mustard 1 tsp

smoked garlic 2 cloves, chopped or **unsmoked garlic**, 1 clove, chopped

flat-leaf parsley leaves a small bunch, roughly chopped

Gruyère 50g, grated

■ Heat the oven to 180C/fan 160C/gas 4. Simmer the potatoes in boiling salted water for 5 minutes, drain and slice. Meanwhile, fry the mushrooms in a little olive oil with the bay leaf until golden and all the moisture has bubbled off. Layer the potatoes in a buttered baking dish with the mushrooms.

■ Mix the cream, milk, mustard, garlic and parsley together and season. Pour over the potatoes and mushrooms, sprinkle the Gruyère over and bake for 30–40 minutes, until the potatoes are tender and the top is golden.

Any good melting cheese will work here. Try Emmenthal or Comte.

Coq au vin with pommes Voisin

1½ hours

olive oil

unsalted butter 25g

thick-cut back bacon 4 rashers or
    pancetta, 75g, cut into 1cm cubes

small pickling onions 350g, peeled

garlic 6 cloves, sliced

whole chicken 1.5–2kg, cut into 8 pieces,
    or 8 **chicken pieces**

flour 2 tbsp, seasoned

red wine 600ml

redcurrant jelly 1 tbsp

bay leaf 1

fresh rosemary a sprig

flat-leaf parsley a small bunch, finely
    chopped, plus extra for decoration

sage leaves small bunch

button chestnut mushrooms 175g

POMMES VOISIN

butter 75g, melted, plus extra for greasing

small waxy potatoes such as Charlotte or
    Anya 750g, sliced as thick as a £1 coin

parmesan 25g, freshly grated

■ Heat the oven to 200C/fan 180C/gas 6. Heat 1 tbsp oil and the butter in a casserole and cook the bacon and onions for 5 minutes until golden, then add the garlic and cook briefly. Remove.

■ Dust the chicken with flour. Fry until golden brown. Put the chicken and bacon back in the casserole with the wine and redcurrant jelly. Bring to the boil. Tie the herbs up and add to the pan. Season, cover and cook in the oven for 1 hour. After 30 minutes add the mushrooms.

■ For the pommes Voisin, generously butter a 15cm-round cake tin and layer the potatoes in the bottom. Drizzle with melted butter, sprinkle with parmesan and season. Continue until all the potatoes have been used. Cook alongside the chicken for about 40–50 minutes or until tender. Unmould on to a plate.

■ Remove the chicken, keep warm and boil the remaining sauce for 5 minutes until reduced. Serve together. **Serves 4**

To get the chicken nicely golden brown, fry 2 or 3 pieces at a time and don't overcrowd the pan.

Double cheese soufflés

40 minutes

butter 25g, plus extra for greasing
flour 25g
milk 250ml
soft goat's cheese 100g, crumbled
parmesan 50g, grated
fresh chives chopped to give 2 tbsp
eggs 5, separated

Don't be tempted to look in the oven until the cooking time is up as the soufflés could collapse.

■ Heat the oven to 200C/fan 180C/gas 6. Butter 4 × 250ml soufflé dishes. Melt the butter in a saucepan, stir in the flour and cook for a minute or so. Slowly add the milk, stirring all the time to make a thick sauce. Cook for a couple of minutes to get rid of the floury taste. Stir in the cheeses and chives then add 4 of the egg yolks, season generously and mix well.

■ In a clean bowl, whisk all the egg whites until they are stiff and form soft peaks. Carefully fold the egg whites into the cheese mixture and pour into the buttered soufflé dishes. Cook for 12–15 minutes until the soufflés are risen and golden. **Serves 4**

Toulouse sausage and butter bean casserole

40 minutes

sausages 6 spicy ones, Toulouse are good
olive oil for frying
streaky bacon 6 slices, chopped
leek 1 large, sliced
garlic 1 clove, sliced
white wine 1 large glass
chicken stock fresh, cube or concentrate, made up to 200ml
dried chilli flakes a pinch
butter beans 2 × 400g tins, drained and rinsed
parsley leaves a small bunch, roughly chopped

■ Brown the sausages in a little oil. Scoop out and slice into chunks. Brown the bacon in the same pan then add the leek and garlic and cook until softened. Return the sausages to the pan and add the wine, stock, chilli flakes and butter beans. Simmer for 10–15 minutes until the sausages are cooked through. Season and add the parsley. **Serves 4**

Butter beans are also known as lima beans – they come dried, in tins or in jars.

French onion soup

1 hour

butter 50g
onions 1 kg, thinly sliced
thyme leaves 2 tbsp
dry sherry 3 tbsp
beef stock fresh, cube or concentrate,
    made up to 1.2 litres

CROUTONS
baguette 1, sliced
garlic 1 clove, halved
extra-virgin olive oil for drizzling
Gruyère 100g, grated

■ Heat the butter in a large pan and gently cook the onion and thyme until the onion is softened but not browned – about 20 minutes. Increase the heat slightly and cook for 15 minutes, until the onion becomes dark golden, sticky and caramelized, stirring now and again to stop it catching.

■ Add the sherry and simmer for 2–3 minutes, then add the stock and bring to the boil. Season. Simmer for 10 minutes.

■ Meanwhile, toast the bread, rub each slice with garlic, then drizzle with a little oil. Sprinkle with the cheese and grill until golden and bubbling. Serve the soup with the cheese croutons on top. **Serves 4**

Ordinary brown onions are best for this. Red onions will go an unappetizing grey colour as they cook.

Grilled crottin with pear and walnut salad

10 minutes

goat's cheese crottin 1, halved horizontally

sherry vinegar 1 tbsp

walnut oil 4 tbsp

salad leaves 2 handfuls

ripe pear 1, peeled and halved or quartered

walnut halves 10, toasted

■ Heat the grill to high and grill the cheese, cut-side up, until browned. Whisk together the sherry vinegar and walnut oil to make a dressing.

■ In a bowl, toss the salad leaves, pear, walnuts and dressing, then arrange on 2 plates. Top each salad with the grilled cheese and serve. **Serves 2**

Crottins are small, squat, barrel-shaped cheeses with a whitish (bloomy) rind.

Cured salmon with cucumber salad

20 minutes + 48 hours curing

black peppercorns 2 tsp
fennel seeds 2 tsp
juniper berries 4
coarse sea salt 100g
granulated sugar 75g
lemon 1, zested
fresh dill chopped to make 2 tbsp
salmon fillet 1.5kg, skin on
vodka 6 tbsp
crème fraîche and **rye bread** to serve

CUCUMBER SALAD
cucumber 1, cut in half lengthways,
    seeds scooped out and sliced
fresh dill chopped, to make 2 tbsp
golden caster sugar 2 tsp
white wine vinegar 2 tbsp
yellow mustard seeds 2 tsp
olive oil 2 tbsp

Get the freshest salmon you can for this recipe and ask the fishmonger to remove the scales and pin bones for you.

■ Crush the peppercorns, fennel seeds and juniper berries in a pestle and mortar. Add the salt, sugar, lemon zest and dill and mix. Put 2 large pieces of foil on top of each other on a baking tray and scatter ⅓ of the salt mix into the middle.

■ Cut the salmon fillet into two pieces. Lay 1 piece skin-side down on top of the salt. Scatter with another ⅓ of the salt mix and ½ of the vodka, then lay the other piece skin-side up on top and scatter with the remaining salt mixture and vodka. Wrap tightly in the foil, put a heavy chopping board on top and chill for 2 days, turning it every 12 hours and tipping off any liquid.

■ To make the salad, scatter the cucumber with 2 tsp salt, mix and leave for 1 hour in a colander. Rinse and pat dry with kitchen paper. Whisk the remaining ingredients and pour over the cucumber.

■ To serve the salmon, scrape off as much salt as possible and lay the fillets skin-side down on a board. Cut thin slices from each piece and arrange on a platter. Serve with the cucumber salad, rye bread and crème fraîche. **Serves 6**

Pork and veal terrine with pistachios

20 minutes + 1 ¼ hours in the oven

butter 50g

onion, 1 finely chopped

garlic 2 cloves, finely chopped

fennel seeds 1 tbsp

pork 1 kg, minced or diced

brandy 4 tbsp

lemons 3, zest only

thyme leaves 4 tbsp

shelled pistachio nuts 75g

eggs 1

unsmoked streaky bacon rashers 12

fresh chives a small bunch

veal escalope 200g

If you want a smoothish texture for your terrine, buy minced pork. Or dice a piece of pork (choose a cut like shoulder with some fat on it) if you would like a rougher, more rustic, end result.

■ Heat the oven to 180C/fan 160C/gas 4. Melt the butter in a frying pan and cook the onion and garlic until soft. Add the fennel seeds and stir briefly. Cool.

■ Mix the pork with the brandy, lemon zest, thyme, pistachios and onion mixture. Season well. Fry a little piece of the mixture to taste it and add more seasoning if you need to. Add the egg and mix well.

■ Butter a 22cm × 8cm × 7cm (deep) terrine or loaf tin and line it widthways with the bacon rashers. Leave the edges overhanging so that you can fold them over the top later. Half-fill the terrine with the mixture and then add a layer of whole chives followed by a layer of the veal escalope (cut to fit if you need to). Fill the terrine to the top with the rest of the pork mixture and push it down firmly, then fold the bacon rashers over. Cover with a piece of buttered foil, folding it tightly around the edge of the tin.

■ Cook for 1 hour 15 minutes. Lift the tin out on to a wire rack, put a board on top to weight it down and flatten the top. When it's cool, turn it out and slice.

Serves 8

Pork fillet with mustard-seed Puy lentils

45 minutes

olive oil for frying

pork fillet 300g, trimmed

wholegrain mustard 2 tbsp

Puy lentils 200g

potatoes 100g, cut into chunks

red onions 2 small, peeled and quartered

sun-dried tomatoes in olive oil 6, drained

fresh thyme 2 sprigs

beef stock fresh, cube or concentrate, made up to 700ml

parsley 3 tbsp, chopped

■ Heat a little olive oil in a deep frying pan, season the pork and spread with half of the mustard. Fry for a couple of minutes until lightly browned all over. Remove the pork from the pan and set aside.

■ Add the lentils, potatoes, onions, sun-dried tomatoes and thyme to the frying pan. Then mix the remaining mustard into the stock, pour it over the lentil mixture and cook for 15 minutes. Top with the pork fillet, cover and cook for a further 15 minutes.

■ Leave the fillet to rest for 5 minutes before carving. Stir the parsley into the lentil mixture and serve with slices of pork. **Serves 2**

This recipe can easily be doubled to feed a crowd.

Pot-roast chicken with Seville oranges

1 hour 25 minutes

butter 25g
whole chicken or **guinea fowl** 1.5kg
shallots 8, peeled
Seville oranges 2, cut into thick wedges
cinnamon sticks 2
honey 1 tbsp
parsley a small bunch
chicken stock fresh, cube or concentrate,
    made up to 250ml
potatoes, rice or **couscous** to serve

Seville oranges have a short season,
from the end of December to February.
Use ordinary oranges when they
aren't around.

■ Heat the butter in a large lidded casserole over a medium heat. Add the chicken and brown all over. Throw in the shallots and orange wedges. Brown briefly, then add the cinnamon, honey and parsley.

■ Pour in the stock, bring to the boil, then reduce the heat to a simmer. Tightly cover with a lid and simmer for 50–60 minutes until cooked through. The juices should run clear when a skewer is pushed into the fat part of the thigh. If still pink, cook for a little longer.

■ Lift out the chicken and boil the liquid rapidly for a couple of minutes, uncovered, to make a syrupy sauce. Fish out and discard the spices and parsley.

■ Carve the chicken, or cut into portions using kitchen scissors. Serve with the sauce, orange pieces and shallots. Goes well with potatoes, rice or couscous.

Serves 4

Roast garlic and potato stuffed poussins

1¾ hours

potatoes 700g, unpeeled, diced

bay leaves 8, finely chopped

garlic 8 cloves, crushed

poussins 8

bacon 8 rashers

olive oil

plain flour 25g

vegetable or chicken stock fresh, cube
or concentrate, made up to 300ml

white wine 200ml

coriander leaves a small bunch

parsley leaves 6 tbsp, chopped

lemon 1, juiced

garlic 2 cloves

Serve the poussins whole, or cut them
in half or quarters with poultry shears.
You'll need one poussin per person.

■ Heat the oven to 190C/fan 170C/gas 5.
Cook the potatoes in boiling water for
3 minutes. Drain well. Stir in the bay
leaves and crushed garlic. Season well
with salt and pepper.

■ Remove any string from the poussins
and trim excess skin from the necks.
Stuff with the potato mixture and
season well. Drape a rasher of bacon
over each poussin.

■ Put a little oil in a large roasting
tin, add the poussins and roast for
40 minutes until cooked. Check by
pushing a skewer into one of the thighs;
when ready, the juices will run clear.
Remove from the tin and keep warm.

■ Sprinkle the flour into the tin and mix
well. Whisk in the stock and wine. Bring
to the boil over a low heat, whisking
constantly. Simmer for about 2 minutes
until the sauce has thickened a little.
Strain and keep warm. Whiz the
coriander, parsley, lemon juice and garlic
with 5 tbsp olive oil. Serve the poussin
with the sauce and the herby oil. **Serves 8**

Steak au poivre

20 minutes

black, green or **mixed peppercorns** 1 tbsp,
    crushed using a pestle and mortar
sirloin steaks 2, about 175g each, choose
    steak with a nice marbling of fat
    through it
butter 1 tsp
brandy 2 tbsp
red wine 2 tbsp
whipping cream 4 tbsp

Timings for cooking steak depend on
the thickness, so test by touch. Raw steak
will feel like a soft pillow; rare steak is
bouncier, like a soft mattress. Medium
will be springy, and well done has very
little give at all.

■ Press the crushed peppercorns into
both sides of the steak, to coat it evenly.
Leave to come up to room temperature.
■ Heat a large frying pan over a medium-
high heat and add the butter. When it
is foaming, sprinkle the steaks with
salt and put them in the pan. Cook for
2 ½ minutes, then turn and cook for a
further 2 ½ minutes on the other side
for rare (add another minute each side for
medium-rare and 2 minutes for medium).
■ Tip in the brandy, allowing it to bubble
up for a couple of minutes. Take out the
steaks and rest on hot plates.
■ Add the wine to the pan, scraping to
get up all the sticky, caramelized meat
juices. Stir in the cream, bubble gently
until thickened. If it separates and looks
curdled, add a bit of water and stir
vigorously; it'll come together nicely.
Serve the steaks on warm plates with the
sauce spooned over and with chips and
roasted vine tomatoes on the side.
Serves 2

Stick-to-your-ribs tartiflette

1 hour

waxy potatoes 750g, such as Desirée or
    Estima, peeled and thickly sliced
bacon lardons or cubetti di
    pancetta 200g
olive oil for frying
onions 2, halved and thinly sliced
butter
reblochon or brie 300g, rind removed
    and sliced
double cream 284ml carton

■ Heat the oven to 190C/fan 170C/gas 5.
Drop the potatoes into a large pan of
boiling water – cook for 5 minutes then
drain well. Fry the bacon in a little oil
until golden and crisp. Remove and add
the onions, cook until really soft, about
10 minutes.

■ Butter a baking dish well. Arrange
layers of potato, onion, bacon and cheese
(season as you layer but go easy on the
salt). Pour the cream over.

■ Bake for 30–40 minutes until the
potatoes are tender and the top bubbling
and golden. **Serves 4**

Classic tartiflette traditionally uses
reblochon, a seasonal semi-soft French
cheese. If you can't get it, try a mild
brie or camembert.

The best salade Niçoise

30 minutes

runner beans 100g, sliced
eggs 4
new potatoes 4 medium, cooked
and sliced
cherry tomatoes 8, halved
lettuce a handful of leaves
tuna in brine or **spring water** 400g,
drained and kept in large chunks
anchovy fillets 4
olives 16
olive oil 4 tbsp
white wine vinegar 2 tbsp

■ Bring a pan of water to the boil, cook the beans for 1 minute in the boiling water, lift out and refresh under cold running water. Turn down the heat, add the eggs to the pan and simmer for 5–6 minutes (or 3–4 minutes if you like the yolks really runny). Plunge into cold water. When they're cool enough to handle, drain, shell and cut into quarters.

■ In a large bowl mix together the cooked beans and potatoes with the tomatoes, lettuce, tuna, anchovies and olives. Dress with blended olive oil and vinegar, season and carefully toss. Serve topped with the egg. **Serves 4**

Hand-filleted and packed tuna has a firm texture that stays in good-sized chunks. Most supermarkets stock a speciality brand, either in tins or jars.

Blini with smoked salmon and soured cream

30 minutes

buckwheat flour 70g

plain flour 70g

baking powder ⅓ tsp

dried yeast ⅓ tsp

milk 175ml, warmed

egg 1, separated

butter 1 tsp of melted, plus extra
    for frying

smoked salmon to serve

soured cream to serve

■ Sift the buckwheat flour, plain flour and baking powder together.

■ Mix the dried yeast with the milk, then add the egg yolk and mix. Whisk this into the dry ingredients to make a smooth batter. Stir in the melted butter.

■ Whisk the egg white to stiff peaks, then gently fold into the batter, keeping as much volume as possible.

■ Heat a little butter in a frying pan and drop in dessertspoons of the batter. Cook until the surface starts to bubble, then flip over and cook the other side. Serve with soured cream and smoked salmon.

Makes approx 30 blini

Try hot smoked trout or Avruga caviar as an alternative topping.

Petits pots au chocolat

20 minutes + 1 hour in the oven

single cream 284ml carton, plus extra
    to serve (optional)
70% dark chocolate 100g, roughly
    chopped
egg yolks 2
caster sugar 1 tbsp
vanilla extract ½ tsp

Vary the flavour by adding 1 tbsp
Cointreau, Baileys or Tia Maria instead
of the vanilla.

■ Heat the oven to 140C/fan 120C/gas 1.
Heat the cream until almost boiling, then
take off the heat. Stir the chocolate into
the cream until it melts.

■ Beat the egg yolks, sugar and vanilla
extract in a bowl, then pour over the
chocolate cream, mixing well. Taste and
add a little more sugar if it isn't sweet
enough for you. Pour the mixture through
a sieve into a jug. Divide the mixture
among 4 small heatproof glasses,
ramekins or espresso cups and put them
in a deep ovenproof dish. Pour enough
boiling water into the dish to come
halfway up the sides of the glasses.
Carefully lift into the oven and cook
for 1 hour.

■ Remove from the bain-marie, cool, then
chill for at least 3 hours and up to 3 days.
Serve as they are or with a little single
cream poured over the top. **Serves 4**

Toffee pear galettes

40 minutes

pears 2 small ripe
ready-rolled puff pastry 1 sheet, cut into
    4 circles
dulce de leche 2 tbsp (or other thick
    toffee sauce)
egg 1, whisked to glaze
crème fraîche to serve

■ Heat the oven to 200C/fan 180C/gas 6.
Peel the pears. Halve and core them then
slice down lengthways leaving them
joined at the stalk end.
■ Lay the pastry on a baking sheet. Put
½ spoonful of dulce de leche in the centre
of each circle and fan a pear out on top.
Glaze the edges then bake for 20–25
minutes or until puffed and golden. Serve
with a dollop of crème fraîche. **Serves 4**

For a crisp base, put the pastry on to
a baking sheet and then that on top of a
hot baking sheet in the oven.

Tomato, squash and spinach curry

30 minutes

onion 1 large, halved and sliced

oil 1 tbsp

Madras curry paste 2 tbsp

butternut squash 1 small, about 500g, peeled and cut into chunks

tomatoes 5, quartered

spinach 500g, roughly chopped

basmati rice steamed, to serve

■ Cook the onion in the oil for 5 minutes until softened. Add the curry paste and cook for 3 minutes. Add the squash, tomatoes and 200ml water, stir well.

■ Cover and simmer for 15 minutes until the squash is just cooked and the tomatoes have broken down. Stir through the spinach and leave for a couple of minutes to wilt. Season and serve with basmati rice. **Serves 4**

Curry pastes come in many different strengths. Check the label and use one that suits your heat tolerance.

Coconut dhal

30 minutes

red lentils 250g
coconut milk 400ml tin
onions 2, 1 finely chopped, 1 sliced
tomatoes 2 medium, chopped
green chillies 2–3 sliced
turmeric 1 tsp
oil 4 tbsp
fresh curry leaves a handful, look
    for them in Asian grocers, or use
    coriander leaves
black mustard seeds 2 tsp, find them in
    the spice section
flatbread to serve

■ Put the lentils, coconut milk, the chopped onion, tomatoes, chillies and turmeric in a pan with 300ml water, season and simmer for 20 minutes, until the lentils are tender. Fry the sliced onion in the oil until crisp, add the curry leaves (or coriander) and mustard seeds and sizzle together. Pour over the lentils. Serve with flatbread. **Serves 4**

Red lentils are also called masoor dal or Egyptian lentils.

Chicken tikka masala

1 hour

chicken breasts 4, each cut into 4–6
  pieces
tikka masala curry paste 1 jar, try Patak's
butter
coriander leaves a small handful,
  chopped

SAUCE
oil for frying
onion 1, finely chopped
garam masala 1 tbsp
chopped tomatoes 400g tin
tomato purée 2 tsp
sugar 2 tsp
double cream 142ml carton
ground almonds 1 tbsp

■ Put the chicken in a bowl and add
4 tbsp tikka paste, mix together well and
leave for an hour.

■ Heat the oven to 220C/fan 200C/gas 7.
Meanwhile, to make the sauce, heat a
little oil in a saucepan and fry the onion
until softened and starting to brown.
Add the garam masala and cook for a
minute, then add the chopped tomatoes,
tomato purée and sugar and bring
everything to a simmer. Cook for 10–15
minutes until the mixture thickens then
add the cream and almonds and simmer
for 2–3 minutes.

■ Spread the chicken pieces on a rack
over a roasting tin and cook for 15
minutes until just cooked. Add to the
sauce, season with salt and stir in a knob
of butter and the coriander. **Serves 4**

Make sure your chicken gets nicely
browned at the edges when grilling
to add flavour.

Indian spinach dumplings with yoghurt sauce

30 minutes

frozen spinach 500g, defrosted and
    excess water squeezed out
gram (besan or chickpea) flour or **plain**
    flour 170g
red onion 1, finely chopped
garlic 3 cloves, crushed
ground cumin 1 tsp
ground coriander 1 tsp
oil for frying

YOGHURT SAUCE
oil for frying
black or **brown mustard seeds** 2 tsp
fresh curry leaves or **coriander leaves** a
    handful
garlic 2 cloves, crushed
turmeric 1 tsp
green chillies 1–2, finely chopped
Greek yoghurt 250g pot

■ Mix the spinach with the flour, onion, garlic, cumin, coriander and a large pinch of salt to make a soft-ish paste (you need to be able to mould it easily), add more flour or water if you need to. Wet your hands and roll the spinach mixture into walnut-sized balls.

■ To make the sauce, heat a little oil in a saucepan and add the mustard seeds, curry or coriander leaves, garlic, turmeric and chillies. Frizzle briefly and then take off the heat and stir in the yoghurt.

■ Heat some oil in a wok or deep frying pan and shallow fry the dumplings in batches until browned all over. They will need enough time to cook through so don't brown them too quickly, about 6–8 minutes per batch. Keep them warm as you cook the rest. Serve the dumplings with the sauce and some naan bread.

Serves 4

Pale-yellow gram flour can be found in Indian shops, some supermarkets and health-food shops.

Fish curry

30 minutes

onion 1, finely sliced

olive oil for frying

curry paste 2 tbsp, Madras is good for this

chopped tomatoes 2 × 400g tins

white fish fillets 450g, skinnned, cut into
    large chunks

coriander leaves a small handful

naan bread or basmati rice to serve

■ Fry the onion in a large pan with a little oil until softened then add the curry paste and cook for 2 minutes. Stir in the tomatoes then simmer for 10 minutes until reduced and thickened.

■ Add the fish and gently simmer for 3–4 minutes until it is cooked through. Scatter with coriander and serve with naan bread or steamed basmati rice.

Serves 4

Use any white fish for this, but check it's from a sustainable source.

Lamb saag

1 hour 45 minutes

garlic 3 cloves, peeled
root ginger large thumb-sized piece,
    roughly chopped
green chillies 2–3, roughly chopped
onion 1 large, roughly chopped
oil for frying
diced lamb shoulder 750g, fat
    trimmed off
cumin seeds 2 tsp, toasted and ground
coriander seeds 2 tsp, toasted and ground
turmeric 1 tsp
cardamom pods 2, squashed with the
    blade of a knife
tomatoes 4 large, quartered
lamb stock fresh, cube or concentrate,
    made up to 300ml
spinach 200g, washed and roughly
    chopped
coriander leaves to garnish
naan bread or **basmati rice** to serve

■ Put the garlic, ginger, chillies and onion into a small food processor and whiz to a purée (or you could very finely chop everything).

■ Heat a little oil in a large casserole. Brown the lamb all over and scoop out. Fry the spices in the same pan for a couple of minutes until fragrant then add the onion purée and cook for 2 minutes. Add the lamb, tomatoes and stock. Stir, cover and cook for 45 minutes.

■ Stir in the spinach then cook for a further 45 minutes or until the lamb is meltingly tender. Scatter the coriander over. Serve with naan bread or basmati rice. **Serves 4**

Buying whole spices means they will keep longer and toasting them releases more of the flavour. Crush them in a coffee grinder or pestle and mortar.

Pea and tomato curry

40 minutes

onion 1, chopped

root ginger a thumb-sized piece, chopped

garlic 1 clove

paneer 250g, cut into chunks

oil for frying

garam masala 2 tsp

turmeric ½ tsp

cayenne a pinch

tomatoes 4, roughly chopped

vegetable stock fresh, cube or
concentrate, made up to 300 ml (or
use water)

frozen peas 300g, defrosted

■ Whiz the onion, ginger and garlic in a food processor until puréed. Fry the paneer in 2 tsp of oil until golden brown. Scoop out. Fry the onion mix until fragrant, about 5 minutes. Stir in the spices, then the tomatoes and stock, and simmer for 10 minutes until thickened. Add the paneer and peas and cook for 5 minutes. **Serves 4**

Paneer is a mild Indian cheese that keeps its shape when cooked.

Prawn curry

20 minutes

coconut milk 400ml tin
green chillies 3
coriander leaves 1 bunch, chopped
oil for frying
onion 1, sliced
root ginger 2cm piece, grated
garlic 2 cloves, sliced
garam masala 2 tsp
ground turmeric 1 tsp
large raw peeled prawns 400g
red chilli to garnish (optional)
lime or lemon wedges to serve
basmati rice to serve

■ Put a little of the coconut milk in a blender with the green chillies and most of the coriander. Whiz to a paste, add the rest of the coconut milk and whiz again.

■ Heat a little oil in a saucepan and fry the onion for a minute or two until soft. Add the ginger and garlic and fry for another minute. Stir in the garam masala and turmeric – the mixture should smell very fragrant. Add the coconut mixture, bring to the boil and simmer for 10 minutes.

■ Stir in the prawns and cook for 3 minutes or until they are cooked through. Stir in the rest of the coriander. Top with the red chilli (if using) and serve with basmati rice and lime or lemon wedges. **Serves 4**

If you don't have a blender then chop everything for the coconut mixture as finely as you can and mix it together.

Spiced chickpeas with tandoori chicken

20 minutes

chickpeas 400g tin

tomato 1 ripe, chopped

young leaf spinach a small handful, roughly chopped

vegetable stock fresh, cube or concentrate, made up to 200ml

korma or **Kashmiri curry paste** 1 rounded tbsp

cooked tandoori or **tikka chicken breast** 1 large

coriander leaves a handful, half of it chopped

natural yoghurt 3 tbsp

naan bread toasted, to serve

■ Drain and rinse the chickpeas. Transfer to a bowl and add the tomato and spinach. Bring the vegetable stock to the boil with the curry paste, immediately pour over the chickpea mixture and stir.

■ Cover tightly with clingfilm and set aside for a couple of minutes until the spinach has wilted a bit.

■ Meanwhile, slice the chicken, then stir the chopped coriander into the yoghurt.

■ Season the chickpea and stock mixture and spoon into two bowls. Top with the chicken, yoghurt and coriander leaves. Serve with toasted naan bread. **Serves 2**

Sprinkle a little water on each naan bread before toasting to really bring them to life.

Spiced salmon with Puy lentils and mint yoghurt

25 minutes

Puy lentils 100g

lemon 1, ½ juiced, ½ wedges

garlic ½ clove, crushed

salmon fillets 2, skinless

garam masala ½ tsp

mint leaves a small bunch, roughly chopped

natural low-fat yoghurt 150g carton

flat-leaf parsley leaves a small bunch, roughly chopped

■ Boil the lentils for 15 minutes until just tender. Drain, then toss with the lemon juice, garlic and some seasoning while still warm.

■ Meanwhile, heat the grill to high. Put the salmon on a non-stick baking sheet and sprinkle with the garam masala. Grill for 5 minutes until the top is golden and the salmon is just cooked through.

■ Mix half the mint with the yoghurt and season. Toss the lentils with the rest of the mint and the parsley. Break the salmon into chunks and toss with the lentils. Serve with the mint yoghurt and lemon wedges. **Serves 2**

You can also use green lentils or black beluga lentils for this – just adjust the cooking times according to the pack instructions.

Spicy lamb with cream and almonds

1½ hours

garlic 8 cloves, peeled
root ginger 5cm piece, peeled and
coarsely chopped
whole almonds 100g
vegetable oil for frying
lamb shoulder or **leg** 1kg boneless, cut
into large cubes
onion 1, finely chopped
cardamom pods 10
cloves 4, crushed
cinnamon stick 1
ground coriander 1 tsp
ground cumin 2 tsp
cayenne pepper ½ tsp
single cream 284ml carton
garam masala ½ tsp
coriander leaves a handful, to serve

Make sure you brown the lamb really
well – it adds to the flavour of the
finished dish.

■ Whiz the garlic, ginger and almonds
and 100ml water in a blender until you
have a paste.

■ Heat a little oil in a large casserole and
brown the meat in batches on all sides,
then remove with a slotted spoon. Add
the onion and fry until browned, add the
cardamom, cloves and cinnamon, stir
briefly then tip in the paste and the rest
of the spices except the garam masala.
Stir the mixture for 3–4 minutes or until
it has browned a little. Add the meat
and any liquid that has come out of it,
a little salt, the cream and 100ml water.
Bring to the boil.

■ Cover the pan, turn the heat to low and
simmer for 1 hour, or until the meat is
tender. Stir every now and then to make
sure nothing has stuck. If the sauce is too
liquid then simmer it with the lid off until
it thickens; if it's too thick, add a little
water. Skim off any fat then stir in the
garam masala. To serve, sprinkle with
coriander leaves. **Serves 4**

Spinach and sweet potato curry

30 minutes

onion 1, finely sliced
oil for frying
Madras curry paste 2–3 tbsp
coconut milk 400g tin
sweet potatoes 2, peeled and cut
   into chunks
spinach 200g, washed and roughly
   chopped
naan breads 4, warmed through

■ Fry the onion in oil until very soft, about 8 minutes. Stir in the paste and fry for 2 minutes. Add the coconut milk and sweet potatoes and cook until just tender, about 10 minutes. Stir through the spinach until wilted. Serve with naan bread. **Serves 4**

Use orange-fleshed sweet potatoes for this to get the nicest colour contrast. If in doubt when buying, just scratch the skin to see the colour.

Tandoori lamb cutlets with minted potato salad

30 minutes + marinating

lamb cutlets 8–12, well trimmed
root ginger 2 tsp, grated
garlic 3 cloves
green chilli 1 large, chopped (and seeded if you don't like heat)
coriander leaves chopped to make 4 tbsp
lemon ½, juiced
natural yoghurt 125g
tomato purée 1 tbsp
garam masala 1 tbsp

MINTED POTATO SALAD
new potatoes 500g, thickly sliced
natural yoghurt 125g
garlic 1 clove, crushed
extra-virgin olive oil 2 tbsp
mint leaves chopped to make 2 tbsp

■ Bash the cutlets between layers of clingfilm until slightly flattened. Mix the rest of the ingredients (except those for the potato salad) and put in a polythene bag with the cutlets. Make sure they are coated thoroughly and marinate for at least 1 hour in the bag.

■ Meanwhile, boil the potatoes for 8–10 minutes or until tender. Mix together the yoghurt, garlic, olive oil and mint in a bowl large enough to hold the potatoes. Season. Mix the potatoes into the yoghurt dressing.

■ Cook the lamb cutlets over a really hot part of the barbecue for 3 minutes on each side, so they are still a bit pink in the middle but blackened around the edges. Serve 2–3 per person with the potato salad. **Serves 4**

Not barbecue weather? Heat a griddle pan until blisteringly hot and cook for 2–3 minutes each side.

Very quick chicken curry

30 minutes

oil for frying
onion 1, chopped
curry paste 2 tbsp, such as Madras
skinless chicken thighs or thigh fillets 4
tomatoes 4, chopped
young leaf spinach 100g
natural yoghurt 4 tbsp
coriander leaves a handful
basmati rice or naan bread to serve

■ Heat a little oil in a deep, non-stick frying pan (with a lid) and add the onion. Fry for about 3 minutes until tender then stir in the curry paste and fry for a minute. Add the chicken and tomatoes and a splash of water, cover and cook for 15–20 minutes until cooked through. Stir in the spinach until it just wilts then stir in the yoghurt and coriander. Season and serve with basmati rice or naan bread. **Serves 4**

If you have a bit more time, you could marinate the chicken thighs for an hour in 1 tbsp of the curry paste to bump up the flavour.

Cauliflower and spinach curry

30 minutes

onion 1, sliced

oil for frying

curry paste 2 tbsp (Rogan Josh paste is good)

cauliflower 1 small, cut into bite-sized florets

ripe plum tomatoes 3, quartered, or use a 400g tin

spinach 100g, roughly chopped

naan bread to serve

■ Fry the onion in 2 tbsp oil until soft and golden – about 7 minutes. Add the curry paste and cook for a couple of minutes until fragrant.

■ Throw in the cauliflower, tomatoes and 300ml water then bring to a gentle simmer for 10–15 minutes until the tomatoes have broken down and the cauliflower is tender. Stir through the spinach until wilted and serve with warm naan bread. **Serves 2**

If you don't like cauliflower, you could use large chunks of potatoes instead.

Blackened Southern-style pork chops with mango salsa

15 minutes

chilli powder 1 tbsp

salt ½ tsp

sugar ½ tsp

olive oil 2 tbsp

pork chops 2, thick-cut

mango 1 large, diced

limes 2, 1 juiced, 1 halved

tomato 1 large, diced

coriander leaves a handful, chopped

rocket to serve

■ Mix the chilli powder, salt and sugar with the olive oil and rub on to both sides of the chops.

■ Cook the pork chops for 2 minutes on each side on a griddle or in a frying pan, then turn down the heat and cook for about 5 minutes more, turning once. Griddle the lime halves until caramelized.

■ For the salsa, mix the mango, lime juice, tomato and coriander and season with salt.

■ Serve with the griddled lime halves, some rocket and salsa. **Serves 2**

Stop chops from curling up in the pan by making vertical snips in the fat at intervals along the length of each chop. Cooking over a medium, rather than a high, heat also helps.

Black bean and beef chilli

2½ hours + overnight soaking

dried black turtle beans or **black kidney beans** 150g, soaked overnight
chuck steak 500g, cut into chunks and trimmed of fat
oil for frying
onions 2 large, halved and sliced
garlic 4 cloves, crushed
green pepper 1, cut into chunks
red chillies 3–4 large ones, chopped
cumin seeds 1 tbsp, toasted and ground
plum tomatoes 2 × 400g tins
beef stock fresh, cube or concentrate, made up to 250ml
cinnamon 1 stick
soured cream to serve
soft flour tortillas to serve

■ Put the soaked beans in a pan with cold water to cover, bring to a fast boil and cook for 30 minutes. Drain and rinse.

■ Heat a large casserole and fry the beef in batches with a little oil until browned all over. Scoop out then add the onions and cook on a fairly high heat until soft, golden and almost caramelized. Add the garlic, pepper, chilli and cumin and cook for 2 minutes. Tip the beef back in with the tomatoes, stock, beans and cinnamon. Bring to the boil then simmer gently for about 2–2 ½ hours until the beef and beans are both very tender.

■ Serve in bowls with a dollop of soured cream and some soft flour tortillas.

Serves 4

Black turtle beans are commonly used in Mexican cooking. Get them from health-food shops, greengrocers and larger supermarkets or use a tin of black kidney beans to speed things up and add them in the last hour of cooking.

Classic burger

30 minutes

lean steak mince 500g
onion 1 large, grated
parsley leaves a small handful, finely
    chopped
ground cumin 1 tsp
oil for frying
burger or ciabatta buns 4–6, sliced in half

EXTRAS TO SERVE
lettuce or rocket
onion sliced, raw or fried
tomatoes sliced
gherkins sliced
Gruyère or Emmenthal sliced
mustard, ketchup, mayonnaise, chilli
    sauce etc.

■ Put the mince, onion, parsley and cumin with a generous amount of seasoning in a bowl and mix everything well with your hands. Shape into 4–6 patties.

■ Heat a little oil in a pan and fry the burgers over a medium heat for 3–4 minutes on each side until they are just cooked through (or barbecue them for the same amount of time). Check they are cooked by sliding the tip of a knife into the middle of each, count to 3 and then test it against your wrist: once it is ouch-hot the burger is done. Serve in a bun with your choice of extras.

Serves 4–6

Once you've mastered the basics, experiment by adding chilli, herbs or garlic to the mix, or try using minced lamb or pork.

Corned beef hash

30 minutes

small salad potatoes 500g, cut into
small chunks
oil 2 tbsp for frying
onion 1, sliced
corned beef 340g tin, cut into small
chunks
flat-leaf parsley leaves a small bunch,
finely chopped
eggs 4 fried, to serve

■ Boil the potatoes until just tender, about 6–8 minutes, then drain well. Heat the oil in a frying pan and cook the onion until softened. Add the potatoes and cook until browned and crisp. Tip in the corned beef and cook until it starts to brown at the edges. Season, stir through the parsley then serve, topped with a fried egg. **Serves 4**

You can smarten this up by serving on a bed of rocket or watercress and topping with a poached egg.

Cubano Libre pork sandwich

10 minutes

---

pork chop 1

olive oil for brushing

ciabatta roll 1, sliced in half

mayonnaise

Dijon mustard

Swiss cheese 2 slices

Black Forest ham or **Parma ham** a few
   slices

gherkins, cornichons or **dill pickle** 2–3

salad leaves to serve

■ Cut the bone from the pork chop, flatten with a rolling pin then rub with oil and season. Grill or fry the pork chop for 3–4 minutes on each side or until cooked. Spread the bottom half of the roll with a good dollop of mayonnaise and mustard, then put the pork, cheese, ham and gherkin slices on top. Toast briefly in a sandwich toaster, or in a frying pan with a heavy pan on top until the cheese has melted. Add a few salad leaves if you like.

Makes 1 big sandwich

Search out rare-breed pork with extra flavour such as Gloucester Old Spot, Tamworth or Middle White to make this the best sandwich ever.

Chunky guacamole

15 minutes

---

red onion ¼, finely chopped
habanero chilli 1, finely chopped
tomato 1, diced
garlic 1 clove, crushed
coriander leaves a small bunch, chopped
avocado 3, chopped into large chunks
lime or **lemon** ½

■ Carefully crush all the ingredients together in a large pestle and mortar (or in a bowl with a fork).

■ Add a little splash of water to make the guacamole less sticky and remember to leave enough chunk to make it interesting. Best served straight away (squeeze over half a lime or lemon to stop it turning brown). **Serves 4**

Ripe avocados should give a little when pressed – err on the side of very ripe when making guacamole, you want it soft enough to crush.

Hot pepperoni pizza

45 minutes

pizza dough mix 280g pack
garlic 2 cloves, crushed
olive oil for frying
plum tomatoes 400g tin, juice drained
   off
tomato purée 1 tbsp
dried oregano a pinch
mozzarella 1 ball, thinly sliced
pepperoni 100g
sliced jalapeño peppers 2 tbsp, look for
   Old El Paso brand

■ Heat the oven to 220C/fan 200C/gas 7. Make up the dough according to packet instructions. Cook the garlic in a little olive oil for 2 minutes then add the drained tomatoes, tomato purée and oregano. Cook for 10 minutes until thick.
■ Roll out the dough as thinly as possible and put on a solid non-stick baking sheet. Spread the tomato sauce over the pizza base then arrange the mozzarella slices, pepperoni and jalapeños on top. Cook for 20–25 minutes until the cheese is oozing and the base crisp. **Serves 2**

The trick to a really crisp pizza is having the oven hot enough. Heat the oven for at least 15 minutes before putting the pizza in.

Open swordfish burgers with herb aïoli

25 minutes

swordfish steaks 4
olive oil 2 tbsp
lemon 1, zested
ciabatta rolls 2, halved
mixed salad 50g
beef tomatoes 2, sliced

HERB AÏOLI
mayonnaise 4 tbsp
Dijon mustard 2 tsp
lemon juice 1 tbsp
shallot 1, chopped
garlic 1 clove, crushed
fresh tarragon, chives, parsley use 1 or
    a mixture chopped to make 3 tbsp

■ Put the swordfish in a bowl and cover with the olive oil and lemon zest. Season.
■ Mix together all the ingredients for the herb aïoli in a small bowl and set aside.
■ Cook the swordfish on a hot barbecue for 2–3 minutes each side, depending on thickness, until it is opaque all the way through. Briefly toast the cut sides of the ciabatta rolls and put on a platter. Top with some salad and tomato slices and a swordfish steak. Spoon on a dollop of the herby aïoli. **Serves 4**

Drop the buns, and this becomes a salad. You could use tuna for this, too, as it has a similarly meaty texture.

Pumpkin soup with chilli and soured cream

40 minutes

pumpkin 1kg, peeled and chopped
olive oil 4 tbsp
red chillies 1–2, seeded and finely
chopped
garlic 1 clove
milk 375ml
chicken or **vegetable stock** fresh, cube
or concentrate, made up to 750ml
coriander leaves a handful, roughly
chopped (optional)
soured cream to serve

■ Heat the oven to 200C/fan 180C/gas 6. Put the pumpkin in a roasting tin, drizzle with the oil and roast for 15–20 minutes, until tender and a little browned around the edges.

■ Tip the pumpkin, chilli and garlic into a saucepan with the milk and stock and bring to the boil (don't worry if it splits). Reduce heat and simmer for 8 minutes. Cool a little then whiz in a blender until smooth and season well.

■ Stir through the coriander, if using, and top each bowl with a dollop of soured cream. **Serves 4**

As well as the classic Halloween-lantern type pumpkin, you could use sweet-tasting butternut squash, or more exotic pumpkins such as Turbans, Buttercups and Hubbards.

Succotash

20 minutes

rindless smoked streaky bacon 150g,
 preferably in one piece, cut into strips
onion 1, chopped
butter beans 2 × 400g tins, drained
chicken stock fresh, cube or concentrate,
 made up to 100ml
sweetcorn 3 ears, cut into fat disks
double cream 3 tbsp
parsley leaves a good handful, finely
 chopped

■ Put the bacon in a frying pan over a
low heat and cook until the fat starts to
run out. Turn up the heat and fry until
crisp and golden. Add the onion and cook
for about 3 minutes, until soft.

■ Add the beans and stock to the pan
and simmer gently until the stock is
reduced by half.

■ Add the sweetcorn and cream and
simmer for 5 minutes or until the corn is
tender. Stir in the parsley. **Serves 4**

Eat this as a side dish or as a main course,
spooned over a baked potato.

Smoked haddock chowder

30 minutes

leeks 3, sliced

onion 1, sliced

butter for frying

potatoes 3 medium, diced

milk 400ml

vegetable stock fresh, cube or
concentrate, made up to 400ml

smoked haddock 500g skinless fillet, cut
into bite-sized pieces

cooked peeled prawns 200g

parsley leaves a small bunch, roughly
chopped

■ Cook the leek and onion in a large pot with a knob of butter for about 5 minutes until they start to soften. Add the potatoes, milk and vegetable stock. Bring to the boil then reduce to a simmer, cover and cook gently for about 10–15 minutes or until the potatoes are tender.

■ Drop in the haddock and prawns and simmer for a further 2–3 minutes to cook the haddock and heat the prawns. Season, add the chopped parsley, and serve in deep bowls with crusty bread.

Serves 6

You can use any potatoes for this. Waxy ones will keep their shape, whereas floury varieties will break up a little and give you a thicker soup.

Smoky chicken soft tacos

15 minutes

chicken breasts 2, skin on
smoked paprika 1 tsp
oil for frying
flour tortillas 4
cherry tomatoes 10, halved
red onion 1 small, sliced
avocado 1 small, peeled and sliced
coriander leaves a small handful, roughly
    chopped
lime 1, cut into quarters
crème fraîche or **soured cream** 4 tbsp

■ Rub the chicken all over with the smoked paprika and season. Fry the chicken in a non-stick pan until skin is cooked and crisp and the chicken cooked through. Pull into pieces. Fill the tortillas with the chicken, cherry tomatoes, red onion, avocado and fresh coriander. Squeeze over a lime quarter, add some crème fraîche or soured cream and roll up. **Serves 2**

Find Spanish smoked paprika in the supermarket or in delis. It's available in sweet or hot varieties, depending on your heat preference – both work well in this recipe.

Warm steak and blue cheese salad

15 minutes

sirloin steaks 2, fat removed
olive oil for brushing
salad leaves 2 handfuls
Gorgonzola or **creamy blue cheese** 100g,
   crumbled

DRESSING
red wine vinegar 2 tbsp
Dijon mustard 1 tsp
olive oil 4 tbsp

■ Heat a griddle (char-grill) or frying pan to very hot. Oil and season the steaks, then cook for 2 minutes each side for rare, 3 for medium. Whisk the vinegar and mustard with the oil. Slice the steak and toss with the salad and dressing. Top with cheese. **Serves 2**

Always rest steak for 5 minutes under foil for the juiciest results.

Diner-style pancakes with bacon and apples

30 minutes + standing time

egg 1 large

milk 250ml

muscovado sugar 3 tbsp

self-raising flour 150g

butter

eating apples 3, peeled and cut into wedges

bacon 6–12 rashers, grilled and kept warm

maple syrup to serve

soured cream or **crème fraîche** to serve

■ Put the egg, milk, sugar, flour, 2 tbsp melted butter and ½ tsp of salt in a blender and whiz until smooth, or use a hand whisk. Ideally, let the mixture stand for an hour, but you can use it straight away.

■ Fry the apple in a little butter until softened and golden. Keep warm.

■ Heat a non-stick frying pan, melt a knob of butter, and drop in tablespoonfuls of pancake mixture. When bubbles rise to the surface of the pancakes and burst, turn them over and cook for a minute or so longer. Keep warm in a low oven while you make the rest. Layer the pancakes with the bacon and apples, drizzle with maple syrup and serve with soured cream or crème fraîche.

Serves 6

Make the batter the day before, if you like. It will keep in the fridge overnight.

Carrot cake muffins

1 hour 10 minutes

light muscovado sugar 100g
groundnut oil 75ml
unsalted butter 50g, melted
eggs 3
milk 2 tbsp
orange 1, zested
walnuts 75g, chopped
dates 75g, finely chopped
carrots 175g, coarsely grated
self-raising flour 175g
baking powder 1 tsp
ground cinnamon ½ tsp

FROSTING
cream cheese 300g
runny honey 2 tsp
orange 1, zest finely grated

■ Heat the oven to 200C/fan 180C/gas 6. Line a regular muffin tin with 10 paper cases or strips of baking parchment. Put the sugar, oil, melted butter, eggs and milk in a bowl and whisk until smooth. Add the orange zest, walnuts, dates and carrots and mix. Sift the flour, baking powder and cinnamon together, and lightly fold into the muffin mixture. Do not over-mix the batter as it should be slightly lumpy. Divide mix throughout the tin.

■ Bake for about 20–25 minutes until a skewer comes out clean. Cool in the tins then transfer to a cooling rack until completely cold. To make the frosting, beat together the cream cheese, honey and orange zest, and spread on top of each muffin. **Makes 10**

You can top the frosting with extra orange zest or walnut halves, if you like.

Blueberry vanilla pancakes

30 minutes

plain flour 150g
baking powder 1 tsp
golden caster sugar 2 tbsp
egg 1, beaten
butter 25g, melted and cooled slightly
vanilla extract a few drops
milk 150 ml
blueberries 100g

■ Mix the flour, baking powder and sugar with a pinch of salt. Mix the egg, melted butter, vanilla and milk and whisk into the dry mix to make a thick batter. Stir in the blueberries. Heat a non-stick frying pan and fry large spoonfuls of the batter mix until little holes appear on the surface, flip and cook the other side till golden. **Serves 2**

Serve hot with ice-cream for pudding or try with thick yoghurt and maple syrup for breakfast.

White chocolate New York cheesecake

30 minutes + 1 hour 10 minutes in the oven + chilling

Oreo or **chocolate-chip cookies** 16
butter 50g, melted
cream cheese 600g
half-fat crème fraîche 200ml
sugar 200g
cornflour 20g
white chocolate 220g, melted
vanilla essence ½ tsp
eggs 3, lightly beaten
white chocolate shavings, to serve

Don't be tempted to remove the cheesecake from the tin until completely chilled as it might cause it to split.

■ Heat the oven to 140C/fan 120C/gas 1. Line a 20cm springform cake tin with baking parchment. Blitz the cookies to crumbs in a food processor. With the motor running, pour in the butter. Tip the buttery crumbs into the tin. Press down firmly with your fingers to make an even layer on the base. Chill.

■ Using an electric mixer or food processor, beat together the cream cheese and crème fraîche. Add the sugar and cornflour. Blend until smooth, then add the melted chocolate and vanilla essence. Stir in the eggs then pour the mixture into the tin.

■ Bake for 1 hour 10 minutes. At the end of that time, the cheesecake may be slightly browned but will still be very wobbly – don't worry! Leave the cheesecake to cool in the turned-off oven for an hour or two, then chill, preferably overnight. To serve, run a knife around the inside of the tin, then remove the outer ring. Top with chocolate shavings.

Serves 8–10

Asian-style brill with greens

20 minutes

---

brill steaks or **fillets** 4, about 175g each
garlic 2 cloves, finely diced
root ginger 5cm piece, finely diced
vegetable oil for roasting
tamarind paste 2 tsp
soy sauce 2 tbsp
red or **yellow chillies** 2 small, deseeded
    and finely sliced
coriander leaves 1 bunch, roughly
    chopped, keep a few leaves for a
    garnish
greens 400g, trimmed and chopped
spring onions 2, shredded

■ Heat the oven to 200C/fan 180C/gas 6. Score one side of the brill steaks (or the skin side of the fillets) with a sharp knife and rub with the garlic and ginger. Lightly drizzle a baking tray with oil and add the fish (if using fillets, place skin side up). Roast for 8 minutes (6 minutes for the fillets).

■ In a small pan, mix the tamarind with 75ml hot water until smooth. Add the soy and half the chillies and gently warm. Remove from the heat; stir in the chopped coriander.

■ Steam the greens for 2–4 minutes until tender. Transfer to plates and top with the roast brill. Scatter with the spring onions, remaining chillies and coriander leaves, and serve with the tamarind sauce. **Serves 4**

Make sure you have scaled both sides of the brill before cutting it into steaks – or use fillets with the skin on, if you prefer.

Beef skewers with Asian salad

20 minutes

Chinese five-spice 1 tsp

vegetable oil

sweet chilli sauce

rump steak 250g, cut into strips

runny honey 1 tsp

white wine vinegar 1 tsp

fish sauce 1½ tsp, plus extra to serve

garlic 1 clove, crushed

mint leaves a handful

salad leaves small bag

cucumber ½, halved, seeds scooped out
    and sliced

spring onions 3, finely sliced

dry roasted peanuts 50g, chopped

■ Heat a griddle pan or grill to very hot. Mix the five-spice, 1 tbsp vegetable oil and a few drops of chilli sauce in a bowl. Add the meat and stir until coated. Thread the strips on to metal skewers and griddle or grill for 2–3 minutes on each side until cooked through.

■ Meanwhile, mix the honey, vinegar, fish sauce, garlic, a few drops of chilli sauce and 2 tbsp oil in a small bowl. Tear up the mint and mix with the salad leaves, cucumber, spring onions and peanuts and add the dressing and toss carefully. Divide the skewers between 2 plates and serve with the salad and a little bowl of fish sauce mixed with chilli sauce for dipping.

Serves 2

You could also use sirloin or fillet steak for this recipe.

Stir-fried teriyaki steak with savoy cabbage

15 minutes

sirloin steak 1, fat trimmed
oil for frying
onion 1, halved and sliced
teriyaki sauce 1 tbsp
savoy cabbage ½, shredded
soy sauce to season
rice or noodles to serve

■ Slice the steak into thin strips. Heat a little oil in a wok. Add the steak and onion, fry, continuously stirring until both start to brown. Add the teriyaki sauce and a splash of water and toss to coat, bubbling off any excess liquid. Tip on to a plate.

■ Add the cabbage to the wok and stir-fry until it wilts. Season with soy sauce and toss, then add back the steak and toss together. Serve with rice or noodles.

Serves 2

Teriyaki sauce is a mix of soy, mirin and sugar. Buy it ready-made from supermarkets and Asian grocers.

Chinese poached chicken with dipping sauce

15 minutes

chicken breasts 2 skinless

ketchap manis (Indonesian sweet soy sauce)

red chilli ½ thumb-sized, seeded and chopped

garlic 1 clove, finely chopped

root ginger 1 tsp, finely chopped

lime 1 large, juiced

cucumber 1, cut into ribbons with a peeler

coriander leaves a small handful, roughly chopped

spring onions 2, finely sliced

■ Bring a large saucepan of salted water to the boil, add the chicken breasts, turn off the heat, cover and leave for 15 minutes.

■ Mix the ketchap manis, red chilli, garlic, ginger and lime juice. Lift the chicken from the water and thinly slice. Serve the chicken, along with the sauce, on top of the cucumber. Sprinkle the coriander and spring onion over the chicken. **Serves 2**

Poaching chicken breasts locks in all of the juices, keeping the meat really soft and moist.

Crispy chilli beef with broccoli

20 minutes

oil for frying

thin-cut sirloin steak 300g, cut into
    thin strips

cornflour 3 tbsp

broccoli florets from a small head, sliced

garlic 2 cloves, sliced

root ginger 5cm piece, finely chopped

dried chilli flakes 1 tsp

soy sauce 4 tbsp mixed with 5 tbsp sugar

limes 2, juiced

■ Heat a 5cm depth of oil in a wok until very hot. Toss the steak with the cornflour. Fry the steak in batches until dark and crisp. Drain. Pour off most of the oil and stir-fry the broccoli, garlic, ginger and chilli for 1 minute. Tip in the sweetened soy sauce and lime juice and cook for 2 minutes. Toss in the beef and spring onions and serve. **Serves 2**

If you can't get thin-cut sirloin, flatten out a regular steak with a rolling pin before slicing.

Miso broth with rice noodles and shiitake mushrooms

15 minutes

instant miso soup 3 × 8g sachets (Sanchi brand is good)

beansprouts 50g

shiitake mushrooms 4–6, thinly sliced

spring onions 2, thinly sliced

fine stir-fry rice noodles 50g

tofu or **peeled prawns** 100g

soy sauce to season

sesame oil to sprinkle

■ Put the miso soup mix in a pan with 600ml boiling water and bring to a simmer. Add the beansprouts, shiitake mushrooms, spring onions and rice noodles and cook until noodles are soft.

■ Ladle into 2 bowls. Top with the tofu or prawns and a splash of soy sauce and sesame oil. **Serves 2**

If you have miso paste in your cupboard, it will work just as well as the instant miso soup. Both are readily available from supermarkets or Asian grocers.

Muscovado and five-spice spare ribs

10 minutes + marinating and 1 1/4 hours cooking

pork spare ribs 1.5kg
garlic cloves 6, crushed
red wine 300ml
Chinese five-spice 1 tbsp
tomato purée 3 tbsp
dark muscovado sugar 4 tbsp
soy sauce 2 tbsp
coriander leaves and **lime wedges**
    to serve

■ Put the ribs in a large bowl. Combine the garlic, red wine, five-spice, tomato purée, sugar and soy, then pour over the ribs. Cover and refrigerate for at least two and up to 24 hours.

■ Heat the oven to 190C/fan 170C/gas 5. Spread the ribs out in a large roasting tray and pour the marinade over. Roast for about 1 1/4 hours, turning the ribs occasionally, until the marinade is dark and sticky. Pile the ribs on to a serving plate and scatter with coriander leaves and lime wedges to squeeze over. Serve with plain boiled rice and steamed pak choi or spinach, sprinkled with sesame oil.

Serves 4

For sticky fingers, roll up damp hand towels tightly with a couple of bashed cardamom pods for fragrance, wrap in clingfilm and warm through in the microwave for 10–20 seconds.

Miso aubergine with cucumber noodles

30 minutes

aubergine 1, medium
miso paste 2 tbsp
sesame seeds 1 tsp
rice noodles (vermicelli or flat ones) 100g
cucumber ½
rice vinegar or **cider vinegar** 1–2 tbsp

Miso is made from fermented soy beans and adds a deeply savoury flavour to dishes.

■ Heat the grill to medium. Halve the aubergine lengthways and cut a crisscross pattern into the cut side. Put cut-side down on a baking sheet and grill for 10 minutes, or until the skin starts to brown.

■ Turn over and spread 1 tbsp miso paste on each cut side, put back under the grill and cook for 15 minutes, or until the aubergine is soft and cooked through, being careful not to let it burn. Sprinkle with sesame seeds and grill briefly to brown them.

■ Meanwhile, soak the rice noodles following the packet instructions. Peel the cucumber, then use the peeler to cut into thin strips. Toss these with the noodles and season with salt and the vinegar. **Serves 2**

Pork, ginger and black bean stir-fry

15 minutes

pork steaks 1, fat trimmed off
oil for frying
garlic 2 cloves, finely sliced
root ginger 2cm piece, grated
green beans 2 handfuls, trimmed
black bean sauce 4 tbsp
brown rice to serve

■ Slice the pork steaks into strips. Heat 1 tbsp oil in a wok and add the garlic and ginger. Then add the pork and stir-fry until the pork starts to brown. Add the beans and stir-fry for a minute more.

■ Stir in the black bean sauce and add a splash of water, moving everything around the wok so it is evenly coated. Cook for another minute or two or until the pork is cooked through. Serve with brown rice. **Serves 2**

Make sure your wok is really hot before you start stir-frying, otherwise the meat will stew, not fry.

Prawn, mango and spinach salad

15 minutes

young leaf spinach 100g
cooked large prawns 200g
mango 1 large, thinly sliced
spring onions 2, sliced very thinly

DRESSING
root ginger 2cm piece, grated or finely
   chopped
dry sherry 1 tbsp
orange ½, zested and juiced
sunflower oil 3 tbsp
toasted sesame oil 1 tsp

■ Make the dressing by whisking the ginger, sherry, orange zest and juice and oils in a bowl and season.
■ Lay the spinach in a bowl and top with the prawns and mango. Pour over dressing and fold together gently. Sprinkle on the spring onion. **Serves 4**

You could use cold, shredded chicken in place of the prawns, if you like.

Sesame-crusted pork chops with Vietnamese noodle salad

20 minutes

rice noodles 250g

sesame seeds 2 tbsp

pork chops 2, brushed liberally with oil

fish sauce 3 tbsp, mixed with ½ tbsp
   sugar

lime 1, juiced

basil and mint leaves a small bunch of
   each, chopped

red or green chillies 2, seeded and finely
   sliced

■ Cook the rice noodles according to the packet instructions.

■ Press the sesame seeds on to both sides of the chops. Put the chops into a cold frying pan and cook over a medium heat for 3 minutes on each side until the sesame seeds are light brown. Lower the heat and cook for another 4 minutes on one side. Take off the bone and slice.

■ Mix the noodles with the fish sauce, lime juice, herbs, pork and chilli. Divide into shallow bowls. **Serves 2**

Choose nice, thick pork chops so they don't dry out as they cook.

Szechuan pepper prawns

15 minutes

Szechuan pepper 1 tbsp
sea salt 1 tbsp
Chinese five-spice 1 tbsp
groundnut oil 2 tbsp
raw tiger prawns 16, heads removed,
    shell on

■ Grind the Szechuan pepper, salt and five-spice in a pestle and mortar. Heat the oil in a wok until almost smoking. Throw in the prawns and quickly stir-fry until pink and very crisp. Pour off any excess oil, then add 2 tsp of the spice mix and stir-fry for 30 seconds. Serve with extra spice mix for dipping. **Serves 2**

Look for organic or sustainably farmed tiger prawns from Ecuador or Madagascar.

Stir-fry vegetables with cashews

20 minutes

vegetable oil 2 tbsp

red onion 1, sliced

red pepper 1, sliced

mushrooms 200g, sliced

pak choi 2 heads, cut into quarters

garlic 1 clove, crushed

cashew nuts 100g

soy sauce, sesame oil, chilli sauce to
    drizzle (optional)

■ Heat the oil in a wok or large pan. Add the onion and cook for 2 minutes. Add the red pepper and mushrooms and cook for 3 minutes, stirring frequently. Add the pak choi and garlic, mix well and serve with a drizzle of soy, sesame oil or chilli sauce, if you like. **Serves 2**

Pak choi is also sold as bok choi or choy.

Thai salmon with cucumber and dipping sauce

30 minutes + marinating

salmon fillets 4

red chilli 1, seeded and finely chopped

garlic 2 cloves, finely chopped

coriander leaves a handful, roughly chopped

fish sauce 1 tbsp

sesame oil 1 tbsp

runny honey 2 tbsp

cucumber ¼, diced

red onion ½, diced

sweet chilli sauce 4 tbsp, mixed with a squeeze of lime juice

■ Put the salmon in a bowl with the chilli, garlic, coriander, fish sauce, sesame oil and honey. Season with pepper and refrigerate for at least 20 minutes or overnight.

■ Grill the salmon until it is crisp at the edges. If you like it cooked all the way through rather than rare in the middle then keep cooking until the fish feels very firm to the touch. Serve with the cucumber and onion sprinkled over and the sweet chilli dipping sauce. **Serves 4**

The marinade also works on chicken breasts, white-fish fillets and even steaks.

Thai green chicken curry

20 minutes

oil 1 tbsp

skinless chicken breasts 4 small, thinly sliced

green curry paste 1–2 tbsp, depending on how hot you like it

coconut milk 400ml tin

green beans 100g, trimmed

courgette 1 small, halved lengthways and thinly sliced on the diagonal

lime 1, juiced

coriander leaves a handful

■ Heat a large saucepan and add the oil. Cook the chicken for 3 minutes until it starts to brown. Add the curry paste and cook, stirring, for 1 minute until fragrant. Then add the coconut milk, stir and reduce the heat to a gentle simmer. Cook for 10 minutes, then add the beans and courgette. Cook for 3 minutes until the vegetables and just tender.

■ Remove from heat and season to taste with lime juice and stir through the coriander. Serve with steamed rice. **Serves 4**

You can use half-fat coconut milk for this if you want to cut the calories.

Tuna with wasabi noodles

15 minutes

tuna steaks 2 × 150g

noodles 150g, of whatever kind you like best

wasabi paste ½ tsp

soy sauce 1 tbsp

lemon 1, juiced

spring onions 4, sliced

rocket 50g

■ Heat a griddle (char-grill) or non-stick pan and, when very hot, add the tuna and sear on each side: 2 minutes for rare, 4 minutes for medium.

■ Cook the noodles according to the packet instructions. Mix the wasabi, soy sauce and lemon juice together until smooth, then toss through the noodles with the spring onion and rocket. Slice the tuna and serve with the noodles.

Serves 2

Wasabi paste is often called 'Japanese horseradish' because of its heat. Add a little more if you like a bit of a kick to your noodles.

Ginger and chilli salmon in a parcel

20 minutes

salmon fillets 2
root ginger 1cm piece, grated
spring onions 2, finely sliced
soy sauce to season
chilli oil to season
coriander leaves a handful, to serve
basmati rice steamed, to serve

■ Heat the oven to 200C/fan 180C/gas 6. Put each salmon fillet in the middle of a piece of baking parchment or foil. Put some ginger and spring onion on top of each then add a few drops of soy sauce and chilli oil.

■ Fold the parchment into parcels around the fish, put on a baking sheet and cook in the oven for 10 minutes. Open the parcels, sprinkle over some coriander and serve with basmati rice.

Serves 2

If you don't want heat, try a few drops of sesame oil instead of chilli oil.

Vietnamese grilled chicken in lettuce parcels

30 minutes

skinless chicken thigh fillets 500g, pulsed to mince in a food processor or use **chicken mince**

shallots 3, finely chopped

garlic 3 cloves, finely chopped

lemon grass 3 stalks, finely chopped

cornflour 1 ½ tsp

coriander leaves a small bunch, finely chopped

fish sauce 3 tbsp (available from most supermarkets)

golden caster sugar for coating

little gem lettuce to serve

cucumber ½ small, diced

red chilli 1, finely sliced

sweet chilli sauce to serve

■ Heat the oven to 200C/fan 180C/gas 6. Mix the chicken, shallots, garlic, lemon grass, cornflour, coriander and fish sauce in a bowl with some black pepper. With lightly oiled hands, shape the mixture into 4cm meatballs. Roll each meatball in sugar and put on a baking tray lined with foil. Bake for 15 minutes, shaking the pan a couple of times to coat evenly with the sugary caramel.

■ To serve, put a meatball on a lettuce leaf and sprinkle with cucumber, coriander and chilli. Serve with a bowl of sweet chilli dipping sauce. **Makes about 30 meatballs**

These meatballs can be made the night before then rolled in sugar and cooked before serving.

Index

Picture credits and recipe credits

BBC Books and **olive** would like to thank the following for providing photographs. While every effort has been made to trace and acknowledge all photographers, we would like to apologise should there be any errors or omissions.

Iain Bagwell p143, p151, p195, p197; Peter Cambell Saunders p163; Peter Cassidy p4, p35, p59, p69, p71, p109, p101, p113, p125, p127, p135, p173, p147, p199, p201, p203, p207; Jean Cazals p43, p27, p45; Brent Darby p4, p65, p183; Gus Filgate p55, p155, p171, p189; Lisa Linder p93; Jason Lowe p141, p149, p167; Geoff Lung p175; David Munns p47, p49, p65, p89, p129, p177, p185, p187; Noel Murphy p31, p99; Myles New p11, p19, p51, p81, p85, p107, p115, p137, p169, p153, p157; Michael Paul p13, p29, p33, p79, p131, p181, p193; William Reavell p21, p205; Howard Shooter p37, p39; Roger Stowell p4, p6, p17, p75, p83, p117, p119, p179; Simon Walton p23, p53, p63, p111, p121, p191, p209, p211; Philip Webb p4, p15, p25, p41, p57, p61, p67, p73, p77, p86, p95, p97, p105, p159, p161; Simon Wheeler p91, p103, p123, p133, p139, p145

All the recipes in this book have been created by the editorial team at BBC **olive magazine**.